PAST
PRESENT
TO
ETERNITY

Book 3

BARRY H. MANSFIELD

Trafford rev. 11/26/2021

Trafford PUBLISHING® **www.trafford.com**
North America & international
toll-free: 844-688-6899 (USA & Canada)
fax: 812 355 4082

Contents

What to do

by Barry H Mansfield

—◆◆◆◆◆—

It may well be true, that we may face the slings and arrows of outrageous fortune
and we might well be tempted to run away and hide pretend like it's not happening
but I believe and conceive that this method of dealing with life will get you nowhere
so, my suggestion is take responsibility for the direction of your life
forgive yourself for what you perceive as your detrimental aspects
and begin to contemplate the meaning of compassion
as it relates to yourself and others
and I believe you will find that you can gain peace of mind
once you can perceive and believe
that you alone, are in control
and that you can set the final goal
which makes you one with the whole
that lets you know
you are soul

True Love

By Barry H Mansfield

‹•✦✦✦•›

True love is an act of compassion and understanding
it puts no demands on others
and can truly never be expressed with words
it cannot be bought or sold
and must be given voluntarily not under duress or fake guilt
I have sympathy for the misery you cause yourself
I wish you well
but through your actions you cause yourself pain
this doesn't have to be, you can be free
of karmas exacting penalty
it's simple, just learn to be nice you'll see
I has been fun, now it's done to you I say ado
Thank you for the diversion
One More time

To take it back

by Barry H Mansfield

◆◆◆◆◆

I don't agree to be a slave of this insanity
waves of possibilities I can see
the reasons are simple the choices are vast
these moments in time, they are mine
I want my freedom back, I will not let insane malevolent beings
decide for me the path That I will take
I will awake, disregard their horrendous lies
this puppet is cutting its strings
I will keep on loving or at least I'll try
I won't even try to explain what's happening or why
it's up to you to figure that out
I refuse to listen to your screaming and yelling and the way you shout
you can be a puppet and a fool, quite frankly it's up to you
but I will try with all my might to stop this craziness, clear my site
if we stick together and love and care
will break their hold, and be able to breathe fresh clean air
live in a society that is just and fair
I don't know about you, but I care.

There is a problem

by Barry H Mansfield

Unrelenting desperation, cruelty, massive frustrations
flow across our nation like jagged strikes of lightning
it breaks upon our cities and strikes them in waves of destructive mayhem
the voices of our people must be heard and recognized
at the same time, the evil ignorant devastatingly repulsive
segments of society must be put in check, be recognized
for what they are, purged from the processes the righteous
are striving to bring about to reach a fair and just society.
There should be no place for ignorance and hate
good and decent souls should not have to wait
to enjoy respect and understanding,
it is the greed of ignorance and power that must be addressed
so, the laws of love can be observed
and all our people may be truly blessed

Teachers

(What a change from when I was young)
by Barry H Mansfield

———— ✦✦✦✦✦ ————

Of late I have found a group of individuals
that possess compassionate understanding
they are kind and warm and help fill my soul with knowledge
and not just me, all who come in contact with them
feel their sublime grace
what a blessing it has been, to experience their patience
As far as I can see, all, who come within their realm
our blessed by these individuals,
yes, it's their profession but they give their very souls
to this endeavor
I see the wear and tear of this great undertaking
the sacrifice, that constant giving does reflect
pressures and burdens placed upon them each and every day
show the strength of their character
a commitment from which they don't run away,
so, I write this little message
for everyone they have touched
to express the gratitude of all, and how this means,
so much!

Metamorphosis

by Barry H Mansfield

✦✦✦✦✦✦✦

As the mountain flows through times expanse,
it is shaken by the turbulence of existence, and crumbles
in jagged pieces into the river of eternity.
As a river flows around each fragment the rough edges of each, are
Refined, and polished to reflect the light of creation,
becoming the epitome of its perfection
reflecting the essence of its beauty.
Freed from its matrix the diamond within
exposes its true perfection
allowing the light of its inner love to radiate in all its splendor
on all the conceptions of its timeless creator

I see and I hope

by Barry H Mansfield

◆◆◆◆◆◆

Beware you despots, you think you're safe behind your goons
remember how your kind came into power
the reality is when the people, the masses, finally decide
they have had enough of your anti-productive crap
they will rise up and the weight of those masses
will crush you like it did those who preceded you
I see the world waking up again, from its long bad dream
I see millions of individuals protesting in the streets
and it's true that the causes are different
because there are so many unrighteous things that are happening
all over, our pebble in space
but the fact is we are waking up!
Having woken from our dreams we become aware
so, beware you despots
no matter how many you kill or imprison
the weight of the world is upon you
you will be crushed, by the weight of the masses
I only hope that those who take power from you
can find a better way
let us pray.

Freedom

by Barry H Mansfield

+ + + + + + +

Friends of freedom here me
who out there, can see the day when all children can play
allowed to learn in a productive way
although hate and misery are
it's not the way to want it to be
there should be no fear of bombs and missiles that might fall
or worry about the possibility of losing all they love
all they have ever known
leaving them all, alone, scared, and frightened
with no hope.
Friends of freedom please hear me
let us work to bring about a new reality
where love and wisdom are the norm
so, all children can feel safe and warm
still understanding that bad things can be
but free from eminent fear of the possibility
friends of freedom please help me
to make this world as it can be.

Enough

by Barry H Mansfield

✦ ✦ ✦◆✦ ✦ ✦

Enough! Enough! All right already!
I am disgusted beyond words
so much greed and ignorance
parents hating their children, children hating their parents,
brothers, sisters, and cousins willing to kill each other
what will it take to bring this insanity to an end
souls, lost in the crazy nonsense of this reality
somehow, they must be reminded, made to remember
that they are part of the source from which all love flows.
Wait, I too must remember
I must alleviate my anger, not feed the fire
truly all I can do is love have compassion
so, through my example, others may see
each individual
must do their part to end this insanity.

Discussions

by Barry H Mansfield

Old man sitting in the mall by the fountain
asking, passerby's "why"
who are you, whom am I
why, why, why
he says, "the unexamined life is not worth living"
wow, what is his seen, what does he mean
you want to learn the difference between physical and metaphysical
that is to say
there is more to life, than what you can hear, see, feel, smell, or taste
more than physical, metaphysical
has to do the soul, parts of life that can't be seen, but can be touched
through the energies of the creation of life
and believe it or not these are the things that mean so much
find them and find joy, contentment, love will be yours
why, why, why
because these are the things you can carry through time
The keys to eternity.

Dinosaurs

by Barry H Mansfield

Dinosaurs did rule the earth, but nature saw they ate too much
the more they ate the bigger they grew
along with their bodies their greed increased
leaving nothing for those smaller than themselves
who in their hunger and their fear
their precious numbers did decrease
but even then, karma was a force
the laws of cause and effect did take its course
so, from outer space and into time
a messenger of fate arrived and only the meek survived.
Yes, they were strong, and they were powerful
but they became too big for their own good
their time was stopped in its course
with ultimate destruction and ultimate force.
Making way for those who had no power
then to thrive and to flower
that was then this is now
something seems the same somehow.

Can it be

by Barry H Mansfield

✦✦✦✦✦✦✦

Can you imagine
Souls have no gender, isn't that a wonder
they're not sexist in the least.
They make the most of whatever body they inhabit
occasionally, souls find amazing happiness in a particular gender
or they inhabit a particular gender too many times in a row
this can cause them to prefer a particular gender
causing consternation when they inhabit a particular body
not of the gender they prefer
this makes the first statement wrong
so, although a soul has no natural polarity
souls can be sexist
oh well, what do I know anyway

Don't

By Barry H Mansfield

Don't tell me you forgot already
That you, really, want to be nice
I didn't think. You got mad
Now we're both really sad
I guess you were afraid I didn't really
Love you
Now we're both really sad
Be nice, I love you

Better I think

by Barry H Mansfield

Better to have loved and lost, then not have loved it all
tis my belief that whoever first said this
was absolutely right.
To experience love, is a wonderful thing
and even if it does not last, it will always be there in your past
though it may have ended with a whimper
its beginning was a grand and wondrous time
a blessing that can stay with you until the end of time
so, cherish the good, forget the bad
keep love's glow, the warmth and wonder firmly in your mind
enjoy the moments of loves first glow
this is yours forever and this you should know
it was better to have loved and lost
that never to have loved at all

Alternate alternatives

by Barry H Mansfield

Alternate alternative reality's, we can choose which way we grow
from the first moment of life's awareness
there is free will, the choices are ours
for sure we may be pushed in this or that direction
by loves sweet refrain or the misery of hatreds pain
yes, it is easy to take the path of least resistance
to be confused by the lies and misconceptions
but I say to you the truth of existence is there for you to see
it is shouted from the rooftops
and although the storms of deception try to drown out its true sound
if you listen carefully, pay attention its truth will set you free
the truth is that it is up to you
to live a life of beauty or tortured agony
take control of your destiny
be the best soul you can be
love and grace can be yours
open yourself up
let love be.

Sea Of Time

by Barry H Mansfield

Moving onward through the sea of time
seeking knowledge of the ultimate divine
a being both entwined in animal and God.
Looking towards the possibility's evolution or extinction
not knowing which we will find
though some may not perceive the swirling eddies of this place
that thrust our growing psyches through torrents of our minds
who we are, what we are, why we are,
these are the questions wrestled with throughout all of space and time
what will we, ultimately find
some claim that all is good, some it's not, others say there's nothing there at all
I tended to think on the cosmic scale, all are intertwined
it's easy to be lost among the torrential storms flowing within our thoughts
these rains of lust, greed, and HATE are the things that cloud our minds
if we could only negate these things
what wonders might be find

Ever onward

by Barry H Mansfield

❖❖❖❖❖❖❖

In the beginning, was the source of creation

unbounded potential

although it can manipulate itself, this, creative force was only one thing

it had the will and desire to create

so, it did

it expanded itself into the universe

time and space became reality

its spores of potential sang the songs of creation

light merged onto the darkness

matter and energy appeared to be

the galaxies took shape

within these, each star created planets

the potential of intelligent life was everywhere

the spores of creation became individual intelligence

each adding to the creative knowledge of the source

it is the future, it is the past

we are part of its creation

moving

ever onward in its creation.

Bon voyage

by Barry H Mansfield

I've talked about the magic, the power, and the treasures
in the vastness of our minds
I've told you that it's there, waiting, for all who seek, to find
but let us understand that one must give to get
one must tear down old fears and worries
and leave the past behind
take time, to let the world slip by, allow your mind to fly
to realms of time and space, that only with perceptions can you see
the place were only mind and soul can be
do not fret and worry if you can't get there right away
imagine that you're moving on your path with utmost haste
do not worry how long it takes or that your time you waste
keep learning to be compassionate and kind
and one day you will see
the power and the magic among the treasures in your mind
it's waiting there for you one day to find

Wonderful perceptions

by Barry H Mansfield
inspired by Mohammed the key guy

❖ ✦ ❖ ✦ ❖ ✦ ❖

Today I was gratified in my faith in humankind
through the kindness and compassion
of two individuals, strangers
who gave relief to the turmoil in my mind
for sure there are differences, I imagine
in the way we perceive the world
yet their acts of kindness and compassion
has verified, justified, and revitalize
my faith in humankind
why
because they went the extra mile
through acts they did not have to do
that showed they cared about a stranger
someone different from themselves
they acted humanely to another human being
this I feel is a most wonderful thing

Three brothers

Id, ego, and superego
By Barry H Mansfield

— ❖ ✦ ❖ ✦ ❖ —

Id says it wants, knows nothing but itself

ego says cooperative participation is a must when others are involved

superego suggest, it's good to give more than you take

they argue and they fight there's really much at stake

for though their three, there only one

unification is a must when sanity's at stake.

Now, Id, being the oldest and kind of tricky at that

puts the pressure on ego, who says, since ego is better than everyone else,

ego has a right to do whatever ego wants

and ego being ego, and really kind of vein

makes a pact with Id to do whatever it will

regardless of superego's consternation and disdain

of things that might happen to others

to cause misery and pain

yes, ego and id

don't care or give a thought

since they are better than everybody else

even if there not too bright

they'll do whatever they like, says, Ego backed by Id

Still, superego knows their wrong, so, just what can it do

Superego has an edge; it has access to knowledge well beyond its years

Only restricted by its own unfounded fears

20

superego knows what it should do to get them on track

in its thoughtful manner, it found a way to save the day

and stop ego and id and their crazy melee

and form a bond of peace and love

it's really simple and it goes like this

sit down, shut your eyes, and concentrate on just one thing

a word or phrase of power

and given time and patience and practiced every day

this will stop the screams and shouts of both ego and id

and in the silence, that is obtained

the three will find a place to be, where all are one

and joy and peace and love can be.

Learning

by Barry H Mansfield

❖ ◆◆◆◆◆ ❖

The way I understand things is that teaching
is a process which allows people to learn.
If this is the case, then why would you want to distract them
from this purpose,
let us discuss one-size-fits-all, this is an archaic process
because one size does not fit all.
Let's talk about demanding notes, from people who can barely write
people who have to think about each letter before they put it down on paper
and I'm not even talking about words I am talking about individual letters
maybe, you can't imagine how hard it is to listen
and write at the same time. Do you really think that's realistic
can you understand that when you over task many individuals
who can barely write
all you accomplish is making them angry, ashamed, frustrated
and all they want to do is runaway. Also, it can cause them to hate you
the idea of school, the idea of learning.
Or is it a better idea to get them to enjoy learning
and actually, accomplish the true purpose
which is gaining knowledge and the ability to use it
I put the question to you
what do you think?

From the past

by Barry H Mansfield

―――――――◆◆◆◆◆◆◆――――――

From the past the future flows
like the withering of arose
what shall be no one knows
entropy takes its course
still. I hope there is more than this
for I believe in the eternal soul
that leads us to a new birth
where once again the Rose will bloom
it's beauty and its youth restored
for from the past the future flows
a fresh new start where hope still grows
like the first bloom of a fresh new Rose.

Learn and grow

by Barry H Mansfield

◆ ◆◆◆◆◆ ◆

Do not be afraid of what you do not know
instead look, listen, think, learn, so you can grow
understand, what it is that you do now know
a new reality in which to grow
follow this understanding, begin to flow into the future relax and go
surpass your limits, become aware
be part of the future
learn to flow.

The truth of love

by Barry H Mansfield

──────◆◆◆◆◆──────

Love is a multi-faceted phantasm
a specter of light, sound, touch and, spirit
it exists freely for all those who are willing to accept it
bestowed without conditions or demands
it is a force of nature, it understands.
Still, sometimes there's confusion about what it really means
and though it is professed, it is not as it seems
some use it as a weapon to make demands on other's souls
in truth it's not demanding, and makes no impossible requests
the truth is unconditional its freedom and its light
that dissipates our fears and allows us to know peace and joy and
learn and grow without the decay of hatreds unrelenting press.
So, give and take it without fear, never be alone
and no, it shouldn't shame or blame, for that is not love,
what it is, is comfort and support
that allows us to be free, and gives us leave to be the best that we can be

Moments

by Barry H Mansfield

✦ ✦ ✦ ✦ ✦

The fleeting moments of our times, how intense they were,
the memorable interactions of our lives
pleasure and pain both there, alas never again
to be
they are gone with only memory to sustain
each moment rare and precious, some sour others sweet
they were there, now only memories,
So, filled with people, and of times.
I rushed from one into the other thinking they would never end,
without judgment for good or bad, I replay them in my mind
the changes that these moments brought, I never could have guessed
the happiness and pain that I repress or gained,
the wisdom and the weight
my mind Soares even as my body is pressed by gravities pull.
I wonder if these same things repeat in each segment of eternity's flow,
to feel the joy and pain to live and love, with new memories there to gain
feeling the ecstasy and the agony of life's tenuous flow
all the treasured moments, gone, never more to be
only memories that took place in space and time
the remnants of moments sublime
truly, this is all that is mine.

Heart ache

by Barry H Mansfield

◆ ◆ ◆ ◆ ◆

My heart aches from what I see, the true shame is we could be free,

Unfortunately, our world is ruled by avarice and greed

because of this very few get what they really need.

I don't know what or how to say, how much I long for a better day

I wish and hope that one day we will see a more productive way

for us to be the kind of people that we could be

were compassion and love are the guiding force

that sets us on a better course

where those who rule will not lie, but deal in truth, and intelligent compassion rains

to heal the injustice and the pain

get rid of all the greedy fools, so that this world will finally be

a place that's good for you and me, and all may live happily

and find the things they really need

a place where the righteous and love will lead

to justice for all, where all will be truly free,

a wondrous place for all to be.

From darkness into light

by Barry H Mansfield

You don't understand, don't bother to find out
and in your misconception, you lose
your awareness is stifled, enlightenment is rejected
love is pushed into the dark recesses of your closed mind.
Yet, light still shines
Working to illuminate your darkness
love deeply, trust your heart and be brave
eternities light, will, shine on you.
Remember,
There's not only one way, but there are also multiple potentials
within these capacities
are unlimited possibilities, of frequency and amplitude
there, is the light
intuitive perceptions
creative potential will show you the way.

Why

by Barry H Mansfield

<hr>

Many ask why are we here?
The reason is simple, the possibilities are clear
each soul as it manifests is given a chance
to learn all it can, and in knowledge to advance
experience all that you can be, or all you will
it can be quite exciting the ultimate thrill
or
you can spend your life in the boredom
go nowhere at all.
You see, it's up to you just where you will go
just what you get to see, how much you will get to know
about love and life about fear and despair
so, as you ask the question, why are you here?
proceed to live your life however you choose
and remember
it's really up to you if you win or you lose.

Unity

by Barry H Mansfield

❖ ✦ ✦ ✦ ✦ ✦ ❖

When I was a child the first thing that impressed me was
the Pledge of Allegiance
and the thing that impressed me the most
were the words
one nation under God indivisible
with liberty and justice for all
I took that to mean that we were one nation
bound together with the single purpose
and that purpose
was life liberty and justice for all
now we are governed by individuals
who would destroy that unity
who spit on the memory of all those who died so we could be one nation
the most awful thing is the understanding
that at this time
we are once again being split apart
North and South, red, and blue, Republicans and Democrats, left and right
these terms to me are offensive
I believe that the only way for America to be America
is with truth and justice and true equality for all our citizens
and that any individual or group who tries to divide us
should be found wanting and be eradicated from existence
to be replace by a truly equitable system
I truly love the idea of one nation under God indivisible
with liberty and justice for all.

Better I think

by Barry H Mansfield

◆◆◆◆◆◆◆◆

Better to have loved and lost, then not have loved it all
tis my belief that whoever first said this
was absolutely right.
To experience love, is a wonderful thing
and even if it does not last, it will always be there in your past
though it may have ended with a whimper
its beginning was a grand and wondrous time
a blessing that can stay with you until the end of time
so, cherish the good, forget the bad
keep love's glow, the warmth and wonder firmly in your mind
enjoy the moments of loves first glow
this is yours forever and this you should know
it was better to have loved and lost
that never to have loved at all

A better way

by Barry H Mansfield

＋◆◆◆◆＋

You may be shy, so am I
don't be uptight and cry, go out, give life a try
climb a mountain, swim in the sea
find out what life can really be
I know it's scary of that there's no doubt
still, you might like what life all about
and just what is that you say to me
I say
it's about really living and feeling free
at least, that's what life means to me.

Backward or forward

by Barry H Mansfield

＋ ◆ ◆ ◆ ◆ ＋

The dinosaurs that feed off the wealth that oil brings
say without their polluting product the world would fall apart
and the sheep follow their lead like a good flock
they cannot see or understand that times do change
once horses were the big thing
and the fat cats who owned the horse ranches
didn't care that people had to walk through horse shit
or live with the aroma everywhere they went
alas the automobile came along
they said this wouldn't do
they said the Cowboys would lose their jobs
oh, what would they do
so many people out of jobs the country would fall apart
then the dinosaurs 'found oil on their ranches
well, the time for change has come again
and once more you hear the fat cats crying
the world will fall apart everyone will lose their jobs
this is no good how can it be same old song, same refrain
Will we follow them like sheep again
Will we really miss the horse shit and its distinctive smell
or will we move into the future
let the dinosaurs go to hell

It's Up To You

From the twelve golden power books

✦ ✦✦✦✦ ✦

There is no chance, no circumstance no fate

That can circumvent nor hinder nor control

The firm resolves of a determined soul

Gifts count for nothing will alone is great

All things give way before it soon or late

What obstacle can stay the mighty force,

Of a sea seeking river in its course

Or cause the never-ending orb of day to wait?

Each well-born soul must win what it deserves

Let the fools talk of luck

The fortunate are they, whose Ernest purpose never swerves

Whose slightest action or inaction serves the one great aim!

Why even death itself stands still,

And waits an hour, sometimes,

For such a will

Equal-Librium

(A State of Balance)
by Barry H Mansfield

◆ ◆ ◆◆◆ ◆ ◆

There is a need, an urgent need
of individuals who understand the concepts of equilibrium
we need them to help heal the wounds of Savage desecration
individuals, who can work with a cooperative and meaningful dialogue
in order to form a union in the way it was meant to be.
A union of integrated, responsible, compassionate individuals
who can further the needs and wants of a rapidly growing population.
There must be a movement in a direction that tends to eliminate
archaic, misguided, self-centered, unproductive practices.
It is imperative that the many become equal to the few
with true opportunity allowing the probability
of fulfillment that maximizes the potential of future generations.
It is imperative that those individuals who understand the concept of equilibrium
be brave stouthearted and true
and for a time step up and for the sake of humanity
give their time and energy
towards a blossoming of a better world.

Ideas in Motion

by Barry H Mansfield

—— ✦ ✦ ✦ ✦ ✦ ——

Creativity is the only means of success, in the quest for reality
you must think ahead if you don't want to be a fatality.
How do you know what you don't know?
This is a true conundrum
Not knowing what you don't know.
You might try keeping your mind open to new possibilities
stop pretending that you know everything that is
don't makeup facts that aren't real
stop your self-righteous in your zeal to make yourself look better than others
understand that you are a human, and what that really means
falsity is falsity no matter how loud you yell
it is from an acorn that the mighty oak tree grows
and the sun doesn't revolve around the earth
and no matter how many people you hurt; these things remain true
so, use the senses you have been given
learn everything you can, about learning everything you can
the essence is clear, have no fear
stop pretending you're more or less than you are
for as much as you know there is always room to grow
knowledge with humility causes wisdom
wisdom causes peace and prosperity
if you only learn, to learn, what you don't know.
(A hint, love and compassionate understanding is A good place to start)

Humanity

by Barry H Mansfield

What does it mean to be a human being
so many things
to be unsure and feel fear
while having the will to persevere
changing anger and hate, too compassionate understanding
to love and care, try to be fair
in the darkest hour of despair
try to remember your connection to all things
no matter what the season brings
helplessness and hope two sides of the same coin
only separated by a fine edge
can be controlled
by the realization of free will
with the understanding that in eternity
all the differences are aspects
of the whole.

Fall from the truth

by Barry H Mansfield

♦ ♦ ♦ ♦ ♦ ♦

Men of honor they claim to be, holders of truth in the land of the free

for shame I cry, how can it be, many, have forgotten their responsibility

the oaths they took ignored or forgotten

the people they are supposed to serve are no longer foremost on their minds

the quest for power or the group that they serve

becomes more than the people they are supposed to represent

their purpose is skewed or badly bent

it cuts into the fiber of our nation as a whole

because of that, society is terribly rent!

Yet, worse than this there lies and power plays

divide us in terrible ways, making hate and fear the rule of the day

and this is detrimental to the American way

this is not the dream our founding fathers dreamt

no, they weren't perfect, but I am sure this is not what they meant

when they formed our nation's covenant.

I would like to believe that what they wrote is what they really meant

that all men should be equal and be allowed to freely pursue life, liberty,

and happiness, without anger, hate, or fear disrupting their quest

and that the purposes of our representatives are the help facilitate this process.

Lesson your karma, Ease your Mind, be Happy in this Lifetime.

by Barry H Mansfield

◆◆◆◆◆◆

This is for those, would like peace of mind
if you take this advice
you might find the world to be kind.

Love can and should be a driving force. Compassionate understanding leads to love. Which leads to productive creativity, productive creativity leads to a higher standard of living. It is my belief that the primary force is the source of love and all that we understand as creation is an act of this love.

It is the driving force that motivates our universe. It is my belief that because we are endowed with the blessing of life it is important to give that love back. Peace will not come through religious practice or a political leader it will not come through arbitrary rules, it will come through the many souls who inhabit this earth through the act of compassion and understanding which leads to love.

Unfortunately, there are souls who for whatever reason choose to inflict negativity upon the world. Life can be hard, yet overcoming hardships encourages creative imagination to soar in many individuals. This enables to us overcome whatever hardships are caused by those who inflict negativity upon others.

What is karma?

Karma is generally known as the laws of cause and effect, but it could more effectively be known as the carrying of information within our souls. It is this information that we carry with us through eternity which in truth causes the cause and effect which are referred to as karma.

Our souls which are a direct conduit to the primary source it carries this karma or information for several purposes. Primarily it is a means for each soul to reunite with ultimate love. It does this by allowing us to experience this physical life's sensations part of which are to realize and correct the negativity (hate, fear, and general animosity towards our fellow human beings) which is a major cause of all that is wrong in our world. By experiencing this and learning that is not the most productive way we thereby increase our spiritual understanding and at the same time increasing the happiness that we find.

How to work with karma

The first thing that has to be done is that each individual design a statement of desire not for material gain or possessions but for the spiritual enlightenment which can lead to true happiness. I have accomplish this by creating this statement which I will admit I kind of paraphrased from someone else's work and have made it my own. It goes like this.

Dear God, who is everything I love you more each day
help me to serve you in the most effective way
help me each day to earn my bread
also, to forgive as I would have forgiven
the things we do each day
thy kingdom come, thy will be done
I love you more each day.

This is mine yours does not have to be so complicated you can simply say "please help me be a better person" just try to make it something that you can dwell upon and remember whenever life is challenging you. And remember to listen and watch for guidance this will set you on the path of love. (Do not let others try to force-feed you their ideas that go against the natural order of divine spirit, through the misuse of the laws, logic, and other means of control.)

How you can achieve your goal

The second step at least as I see it is to develop a method which will allow you to achieve a higher state of enlightenment and help to negate those who would stop you. Again, in my particular circumstance I wrote this.

Compassion is my passion it is the only way to be
I must live within my compassion if I am to be truly free
if I can love all those around me, I can let all of them love the me
so, I will live within my compassion and be truly, truly free
so, you see love yourself have compassion it's the only way for you to really be
yes, yourself love yourself have compassion
and you will, yes you will be truly free.

The above poem is an affirmation of how I began to achieve my goal. Fortunately, it's not necessary to create such a complicated affirmation. Something simple will do just fine such as (Please let me give love freely so that I will be able to freely receive the love given to me.) This is just fine and just as effective, but I do feel it is necessary to create an affirmation which you can keep in your mind and be referred to in times of stress.

The third step in the process is to understand that you as an individual can control your own life. That nothing outside of yourself can control you, yes, things can influence you but ultimately you are responsible for your own action or inaction. Predestination is discussed by many individuals who believe that the creative force which created the universe is in total control. This is a fallacy; (**we have free will it was given to us at the time of creation).** It is true that at each rebirth there is a basic plan, that basic plan was created by the individual soul who's about to live a new life. But life can sometimes be chaotic, undependable, irresistibly devastating, when circumstances warrant each wellborn soul has the ability to adapt to the new situation choosing a more optimum outcome. *Again, we have free will.* And it is we alone who are ultimately responsible for our own lives. It is possible to ask for help and guidance and help and guidance are available in order to receive these blessings one must actively engage in the forward movement of one's life. Again, in my case I wrote a poem. Feel free to use my poems or any part thereof as an affirmation.

The way I think controls my life it cuts much deeper than the surgeon's knife
love is so real you can taste and touch steel, so you know what you feel
yes, life to is real my heart truly beats, and my pulse often quicken
as I run into the nights fears sometime beckon
yet I keep moving on for I know what I am
a creature of God who was spawned from man
now time never stops, nor shall it ever return
so, I looked ahead, and I watch, and I yearn!

And with love and compassion I see myself grow
and though time moves on
I know that I know

This last piece of affirmation is important for reminding yourself that you and you alone are responsible for your fate. It is by truly applying the things that I have just talked about and by putting in the necessary work towards your goal that you will achieve your goal. In this case the goal being an ease in your karmic situation and finding greater happiness in your own lifetime.

Proprietary

by Barry H Mansfield

◆ ◆ ◆ ◆ ◆

Being a human being my first reaction to systematic injustice is
sadness and anger
but being part of the cosmic all I know this is not the most efficient
or expedient reaction
it is my desire to be part of the solution not to fuel the fire of the problem
so, I will dig deep into the being that is my soul
and have sympathy, yes compassionate understanding
for those who in their ignorance commit crimes against humanity
for they have forgotten the meanings of respect and thoughtful consideration
I, will remember, to understand, (that they know not what they do)
and that the meanness and the hatred that they project
harms themselves as much as others
I will have pity, sympathy on their mind-numbing exploitation
and although I will do everything I can to stop their horrendous acts
I will remember that they too are human beings
who are lost within their own fanatical
self-perpetuating, mind-numbing
reality

Freedom

by Barry H Mansfield

Friends of freedom here me
who out there, can see the day when all children can play
allowed to learn in a productive way
although hate and misery are
it's not the way to want it to be
there should be no fear of bombs and missiles that might fall
or worry about the possibility of losing all they love
all they have ever known
leaving them all, alone, scared, and frightened
with no hope.
Friends of freedom please hear me
let us work to bring about a new reality
where love and wisdom are the norm
so, all children can feel safe and warm
understanding that bad things can be
but free from eminent fear of the possibility
friends of freedom please help me
to make this world as it can be.

How can inequality be alleviated in society without dealing with the true cause which is in my opinion universal ignorance

by Barry H Mansfield

◆ ◆ ◆ ◆ ◆ ◆

The subject of ignorance is difficult to discuss because people equate ignorance with intelligence. But in reality, ignorance and intelligence are two vastly different subjects, although they are related. Ignorance can cause an individual to look unintelligent because of the things they were taught or not taught and the manner of that teaching in their formative years that are not in alignment with the arbitrary standards of society at any particular time.

Inequality in society is directly caused by ignorance. Let me define that; I'm talking about a lack of understanding or knowing. This lack of understanding or knowing is not confined to any one segment of society it is in fact rampant in all aspects of society. And by this, I mean the wealthiest and most influential segments of society all the way through and down to the poorest and least affectional members of society. To make this worse even the most *technically intelligent individuals can through their conditioning by society cause them to* be ignorant of many things. So, you see intelligence and ignorance are not the same thing although there can be a perception of lack intelligences that is in reality ignorance.

Now I am a great believer in diversity within our society I believe that diversity allows for many different viewpoints which I see as causing a greater universal creativity. The problem I have is that sometimes diversity means isolationism or one group consciously trying to suppress all other ideas that do not relate to theirs. Such as insisting that they know what is true and real, and they are the only ones who understand truth. Also, that they are generally better than everybody else. This is where major problems are formed when any group within society tries to keep its members ignorant of the beliefs of other segments of society along with the true nature of humanity, through the use of negative propaganda directed towards everybody but the particular group whose using this propaganda to marginalize, vilifies, and generally to claim other groups have faults and that their group does not.

What is the true nature of humanity:

The true nature of humanity as I perceive it, is that given similar circumstances the majority of human beings have the potential to learn and understand anything that any other member of society can. Now, yes within any society there are those who are genius these individuals although in the minority have abilities that the majority of society does not possess. Also, there are those who for whatever reasons have difficulties which make them seem that they are not as able to learn, these are problems such as dyslexia and dysgraphia, down syndrome and other problems that cause them to have difficulties. These individuals through proper education and understanding can be taught to function as any other member society. Also, there are those individuals whose thinking patterns are so different that they alienate these individuals from society. Although even these individuals with love and kindness and proper education can move closer to whatever the norm is in society at the time.

Inequality and its solution

We have talked about ignorance and about what I feel to be the nature of the human beings in the world as individuals and as a whole being a society. I have touched upon the causes of inequality in our society and those around the world. Now, I want to talk in a more specific venue. But to tell you the truth I have great trepidation in discussing specifics on any real situation. Somebody will get mad because they're really not comprehending what I'm saying and more than likely the reason they're not understanding is because of the ignorance that they are choosing to hold onto.

There I said it the ignorance they are choosing to hold onto. I touched on diversity, and you heard me say that it was fine, and it is the same thing with tradition as long as it's productive or at least non-detrimental it is great. But, when a group of individuals hangs on to negativity from the past without trying to move into the future and not understanding, that by leaving go of the old negativity and willfully expecting positive progression into the future, and if need be, by expressing loudly through intelligent protestation those things they feel are detrimental to the well-being of any group within society.

Then, and only then through the use of productive protestation ignorance can and will be turned into enlightenment. By this I mean that people will understand or at least begin to understand that other human beings are hurting.

But this method is only effective if the individuals who perceive themselves as victims are working together from within their own communities. Understanding their own internal problems and fixing them or at least trying to fix them and not denying them, then true equality can be obtained.

I believe that through varied types of educational programs initiated through all levels of society we can and will become a more fairly equally- integrated, stronger more purposeful and peaceful society.

Free will a personal perspective

by Barry H Mansfield

with input from other valued participants

———— ♦ ♦ ♦ ♦ ♦ ———————

Greetings: fellow travelers through space-time. The following narrative consists of my personal observations. So, let's be clear I have no intention of trying to prove the right or wrong of my observations. The purpose of this narrative is to express my personal observations, in the hope that what you read will give you cause to investigate with an open mind.

I am a great proponent of free will, unfortunately, free will used in *ignorance* will not make you happy. Not only will it not make you happy, but it will make everybody you come in contact with unhappy. And to make matters worse this unhappiness can grow Exponentially.

So let us try to alleviate this unhappiness and bring onto our travels through space-time a greater understanding of the appropriate usage of free will. Now, you might ask, or any way you should ask, just what it is I mean by *ignorance*. What I mean by *ignorance* is a lack of factual information on any given subject. The keyword in the last sentence is factual, and this is the difficult part, what exactly is factual or real or the truth.

Some say truth is in the mind of the beholder. This concept allows you to believe anything you want or anything you've been convinced to believe or any deception that has been perpetrated upon you.

In life, there are many fallacies or misconceptions that we perceive as the "truth".

The truth is that from the moment we are born we are being shown what the world is supposed to look like. And sometimes even though our caretakers may have nothing but love in their hearts they are also victims of misrepresentations, fallacies, and or unintentional deceptions. There are also public and private institutions to greatly confuse you and/or try to convince you that what you see and what you feel is not real at best, or at Worst you are wrong, disgraceful, ignorant, sinful, and/ or illegal.

Wow! What a dilemma, how do you respond when those we love or those who are in authority are trying to convince you that something you perceive as a wrongness is in fact right or vice versa.

This is the time when you do nothing, well, not exactly nothing you don't argue, or fight, or get mad. What you do is start a search for truth. If you believe you're right or if you believe that something is wrong this is the time when you can show the world that you have free will. You do this by searching for the truth. And this search may not be easy, nor will it probably be quick. So, you use your free will, do not allow angry, or feel insulted, or strike back at the supposed insult or feelings of degradation that you may feel are being thrust upon you. This is the time when You use your free will to find the truth.

This is not only the proper way to use free will it is the most productive way to use free will. The very act of investigating, researching a problem that you see, even when others say there is no problem, and that you are wrong, this is the time to demonstrate' s your ability to use your free will.

For those who are not following this let me explain again instead of getting angry you maintained your composure instead of feeling threatened or intimidated you believed in yourself and take an action that is of your choosing which is to find the truth. You didn't allow someone else to push you into anger or cause you to lose your composure instead you chose your path or a path of your choosing this demonstrates free will.

Free will sometimes leaves you with choices that are not what you really want, and it may seem that no matter what you do your losing. And you may not be happy with the choices that are available, but the fact is as hard as it could be, you, still have the free will to make that decision no matter how hard or uncomfortable it may be. And in life sometimes hard choices are all we have to choose from but having free will means that we as individuals get to make those choices. Part of the responsibility that comes with one's free will is taking responsibility for one's own actions or inactions.

So, we can, be right, or we can, be wrong but I for one am glad to be allowed to make my own decisions. Whether I turn right or left whether I go up or down whether I move or standstill this is a freedom that I value as much as the life I have to use it in.

Why we do it

by Barry H Mansfield

◆ ◆ ◆ ◆ ◆

Why do we do it. What is it. It is the act of creation. Creation can encompass the act of destruction. It has no true direction of its own, the direction that it takes is regulated by the needs or wants of the organism. The definition of organism is vast and complex. For the purposes of this narrative organisms can be living biological or nonliving non-biological. A nonliving organism can consist of pure energy that has the ability to comprehend its existence. Organisms can be a single cell or a complex society of individual cells or a collection of information that can maintain cohesion.

The definition of a cell in this narrative is the smallest part of an organism. The greater the number of cells or the collection of information the more powerful the organism. The more powerful the organism becomes the more power it wants and possibly needs in order to keep perpetuating its own existence. The words power and energy are interchangeable. Generally, at least on our planet Earth the creation of power or energy is achieved through destruction.

I am not a proponent of our present system for the creation of energy, because this manner of creating energy is wasteful and waste though it is a creation of sorts is a non-productive creation. And in the end pollutes the organism causing its destruction. Yes, this destruction is a form creation, but it is not as I have said productive and leads to the eventual dissolution of the organism.

So, why do we do it. It is my belief that we do it because it is an unconscious imperative of conscious (living biological) or(non-biological) entities to perpetuate itself or their selves.

The question as to when and how this unconscious imperative was impressed upon organisms or the component cells of organisms is a question relating to the beginning of everything that is or ever was. It is presently beyond my sight or understanding.

P. S. And to those who are truthful everybody else's.

The human condition

By Barry H Mansfield
(at least the way I see it)

It's funny and it's sad it can make you happy it can make you miserable. The potential that I perceive in our existence is immense. The possibilities for creativity and to be productive are only equal to the potentialities of destruction and disillusionment.

They say that youth is wasted on the young well it's not really youth, which is wasted, it is the potential to use this time that you have for your own benefit along with the rest of mankind. This is not applied in every case there are some young people who are fortunate enough to fall into circumstances which help them see at an early age the potential that exists.

Unfortunately, there are many more individuals who walk into a minefield of ignorance hatred, bigotry, and the general highly promoted experience of total misinformation. Then there is the idea that some other figure historical, religious, scientific parent or guardian holds the responsibility for what you do. This is not true, people should learn, understand, be taught at an early age that they are responsible for what happens to them. And that they have the ability through their actions or inactions to take more control of their life circumstances.

The problem with this is that people start off totally ignorant and are taught about life by other individuals who are only just a little bit less ignorant. So how you say could it be the responsibility of these children for the things happening to them. Obviously, there are situations, in which a young child is helpless to do anything about. This is undoubtedly true. Things are going to happen to people of all ages which are detrimental which hurt, cause confusion anxiety, and fear. This is why and where education can come into play.

It is really sad that our traditions of ignorance are maintained so steadfastly in our society. This truly makes it hard for any individual to break out of millennium old habit patterns and see the truth, the possibility of a life that can and should be much better.

There are some people who at an early age learn to use the natural abilities nature has given us. Unfortunately, these are the exception and not the rule and this unfortunate circumstance is the bane of most societies. Also, unfortunately, people are comfortable with old habit patterns, and they call these habit patterns which are not necessarily so good tradition or common sense (you got to appreciate common sense which in reality makes no sense at all) simply because this is what people have been doing for a long time therefore it has to be right.

Let's get back to time and age and how after years of fighting ignorance, lies, hatred, disinterest, and a total dampening of the will that leaves you imprisoned in an existence which was forced upon you by circumstances which you feel you have no control over, that in fact is not true. Although, you were convinced by (society) that this is what you had to do because this is what everyone else did and any action or inaction you took that isn't or wasn't certified by the community (whatever that means) has to be bad, has to be wrong, or possibly a sin. All the time that you are following these rules and regulations which generally, no one gave you a reason for why you had to do this or if they did give you a reason, that reason, the reality, was not a reason that was good for you and your life or for that matter anybody else's life. But what it did mean was that those people who were in charge wanted this thing to be this way because that's what they wanted, and it really doesn't matter what anybody else wanted whether it was good or bad for a particular individual didn't make any difference because they were in charge and if you didn't do it their way you were an outcast you were shunned you were humiliated and or hurt in any way, they deemed it to be.

All this being said you finally manage to figure out what is right for you, and you also are able to develop a way that it becomes possible to do the things that you really want to do. And lo and behold what happens your body starts to break down. Your thoughts fluctuate between genius understanding and oh my God I forgot.

You might learn the wisdom of the ages but that doesn't mean you get to get rid of all the baggage that you've collected. I'm not saying you can't get rid of all that baggage but it's really hard to focus on the new understandings you have while you're fighting off all the old things, you really know you don't need. Not to mention the fact that the cellular structure of your body begins to stop functioning or slows down and for the first time in your life you start dwelling more upon the possibility of dying. Added, to the possibility that all the people who you have ever loved in your life have disappeared and that the world around you is changing so fast that it's hard to keep up with.

Even so, all this being true you still have the capability or at least the possibility to finally take control of your own life. What does that mean, it means you can choose to be of good nature you can decide to have compassion on yourself and other human beings. Also, you can work at developing latent creative abilities and at least in part discover that if you take responsibility for what happens to you, you will find that you can make a lot of the things that happened to you so much better than they would have been if you keep believing that someone or something else is responsible for everything that happens to you.

Consciousness

by Barry H Mansfield

✦ ✦ ✦ ✦ ✦ ✦ ✦

Awareness gives a greater choice
free will through time
reality should not be materialistic
it is probability oriented
understanding this potential, I give an oath
to be the most loving, giving, caring
of beings endeavoring to be
a force of ultimate directional guidance.
It is not what you were when you start
it is what you are when you end.

Life energy and healing

by Barry H Mansfield

A redirecting our designing of energies flow
a shifting of the flow of energy in thought and action
can cause a positive or negative reaction
a thoughtful transmutation of energy can cause a multiplication of this flow
that can alleviate sickness and help you grow.
Life is the manifestation of energy
our physical bodies are made of and with it.
The directional flow if impeded can cause a manifestation
of unwanted, detrimental physical or mental malformation
a negative or harmful aberration.
It may not be easy, but it's truly worth the effort that it takes
to think as positively as you can.
To redirect or redesign energies flow.
Change is inevitable which way will you go.

It's how you play the game

by Barry H Mansfield

Fantastical dreams you say they can't be
you may be right, let's, wait and see,
create your own reality, how many do that
you could fall on your face and just go splat
one in a billion, that's a big chance
but if you don't try, you'll never know
just how far you could possibly go
pick a direction, one step at a time
don't be afraid of the mountains you may have to climb
believe in yourself as part of the divine
Commit yourself, put in the time
it might rain or the sun might shine
don't panic it'll be fine
others might say you'll never do that
thank them for their input, do it anyway
who cares if they don't know how to play
it can be work, or it can be fun
get in the race and really run
it's not whether you win or lose
but how you play the game you choose.

Mass psychosis

by Barry H Mansfield

An epidemic can be viral or psychological
which is worse, is purely hypothetical
both can be devastating to the human race
in either case a cure must be found
viral infections are caused by a little bug,
spread through touch or in the air
psychosis's are caused by a human thugs
masters of mayhem who are selfish, greedy with little compassion
both can be spread through ignorance and fear
by people who believe everything they hear
both take quite a while to abate
so let us develop antidotes for both these plagues
one consisting of vaccine
the other massive doses of love and education
I truly believe this is society's obligation

My choice

by Barry H Mansfield

❖ ❖ ❖ ❖ ❖

Greater awareness of passions expressed
in the ever-present here and now
sounds of light that echo through time
enabling understandings of why and what and how
precipitating control of action and thought
developing life's that are more than naut
knowledge is power, for good or for bad
finding greater truth at least more than is had
ignorance is bliss, or so it is said
realization of ultimate truth
is the path on which I'm led
allowing all fallacies to be shed
gaining this truth before life is fled
understanding oneself is the goal that I choose
for the sake of tomorrow if I win or I lose
I'll try for this goal
in enlightenment's quest

The World of my Creation

by Barry H Mansfield

I walked through time and space at my own pace
I've worked with what I had
my creation is neither good nor bad
at this moment it is what I have made it
which means I'm both happy and sad
still, I direct its flow
this, I surely know.
What I've done in this allotted time
is the creation of my desire
now I'm here at this point in time
what shall happen, the decisions mine.
The rush of youth I left behind
the path to wisdom I do find
is closer now than at any other time
shall I yield to my body
or make eternity mine.

Teachers

(What a change from when I was young)
by Barry H Mansfield

———— ✦✦◆✦✦ ————

Of late I have found a group of individuals
that possess compassionate understanding
they are kind and warm and help fill my soul with knowledge
and not just me, all who come in contact with them
feel their sublime grace
what a blessing it has been, to experience their patience
As far as I can see, all, who come within their realm
our blessed by these individuals,
yes, it's their profession but they give their very souls
to this endeavor
I see the wear and tear of this great undertaking
the sacrifice, that constant giving does reflect
pressures and burdens placed upon them each and every day
show the strength of their character
a commitment from which they don't run away,
so, I write this little message
for everyone they have touched
to express the gratitude of all, and how this means,

So much!

Alternate alternatives
by Barry H Mansfield

· ◆ ◆ ◆ ◆ ◆ ◆ ·

Alternate alternative reality's, we can choose which way we grow

from the first moment of life's awareness

there is free will, the choices are ours

for sure we may be pushed in this or that direction

by loves sweet refrain or the misery of hatreds pain

yes, it is easy to take the path of least resistance

to be confused by the lies and misconceptions

but I say to you the truth of existence is there for you to see

it is shouted from the rooftops

and although the storms of deception try to drown out its true sound

if you listen carefully, pay attention its truth will set you free

the truth is that it is up to you

to live a life of beauty or tortured agony

take control of your destiny

be the best soul you can be

love and grace can be yours

open yourself up

let love be.

The reality of reality

By Barry H Mansfield

+ ✦ ✦ ✦ ✦ +

In relation to vibratory status in and of string theory, matter, and ultimate realities.

I

I am not a mathematician but to the best of my understanding everything that exists matter and energy is a form of vibration. Let's see if I can explain this a physical object a rock is vibrating but is not a waveform, instead they are tiny particles that are called strings which are vibrating in the form of a rock in a steady-state vibration which are not exactly stationary but not a flowing wave such as light which can also be a particle or energy wave.

If this first paragraph is not true then everything else, I think or have said is also probably not true. My ongoing assumption is, it is, true and that the following statements are also true, or at least relatively true in relationship to ideas that are comparatively unknown and possibly at this point unknowable. The subject I'm getting to is the subject of alternate realities and the idea that they are simply states of existence that exist in different vibratory states.

II

The intentionality, or purpose with which you express a thought is integral to manifesting a particular outcome. Along with this, positive action in the direction of your desired goal is extremely important. To achieve a productive long-lasting situation a deep consideration of the ideas and outcomes should be contemplated.

Believing in yourself with purpose, and awareness can direct your energies to the outcome you desire effectively ordering the chaos of our lives.

Barry H Mansfield

As time fulfills

by Barry H Mansfield

◆ ◆ ◆ ◆ ◆ ◆

Peace, Love, Joy, and Harmony
is a way to a good economy
love you give, comes back to you
pay close attention to what is true
yes, free will belongs to you
use it wisely, don't be a fool
so far away, yet almost there, hope for the day all may care
water, earth, and clean air
can be there for all to share
peace on earth need not be rare.

Ultra-sensitivity

by Barry H Mansfield
Inspired By Crazy wise the movie

+ ◆ ◆ ◆ ◆ +

You're not going crazy; you don't need to be medicated
new realities are being opened to you
strange and frightening, incomprehensible
at first, but,
you can understand the new vistas that you see
quiet your mind, you will be free
there is help available
it doesn't come in the form of a drug
it comes from beings of compassionate understanding
that can help you grow, learn to know
what it is you feeling and see
you can control, yes understand
this gift of ultra-sensitivity

Relative reality

by Barry H Mansfield

— ◆◆◆◆◆ —

Reality is a state of mind and is relatively real

yet, it really depends on where you stand and how you think and feel

it matters entirely on what you bring into your perceptual field.

Emotions such as hate, and fear will make it dark and cloudy

this will no doubt make you negatively pouty.

Approaching it with joy and compassion will give you reason to rejoice

this is truly up to you; you really have a choice.

How you act, what you think and say will make or break your day

now I'm not telling you what to do or when and where to do it

what I'm saying is that in life flow it's up to you

that you have a say in forming your reality

so, get involved with their ultimate causality

be a success not a fatality.

A personal problem

by Barry H Mansfield

◆ ◆ ◆ ◆ ◆ ◆ ◆

I believe with no reservations that the way I think controls my life.

Also, that emotions are a prelude to thought

and that it is much easier to control your thoughts then it is to control emotions

that are not as easily understood or recognized.

Regardless, I love life's erratic flow.

So, what's the problem

I'm angry at the wind for blowing,

I'm angry with the sun for shining too much or not enough,

I'm angry at the inconvenient rain, that rains on my parade.

Anger, fear, close or the same

emotions, buried deep in my psyche

hard to touch, and harder to understand.

I can hear my thoughts, I can feel their flow

I have the ability to rationally understand if their direction is not where I want to go.

But these emotions are another story

one that's hard to read

I try, but time does fly

So, you see, this is my personal problem.

The beginning of the end of the beginning of the end of the beginning

by Barry H Mansfield

✦✦✦✦✦

In a time before history in a place known but unknown
were men of power whose mission it was the save man from itself.
There were those who had opened the door to a wondrous place,
that could curse or bless the human race to the depths of hell or the wonders of outer space.
Seven were chosen for their wisdom, stature, and grace
for where they had to walk was a dangerous place,
dimensions known and unknown the fastness of time and space
A quest for knowledge. Search for truth.
A productive reality to teach in youth,
a meaningful way to look at life, that circumvents fear, hate, war, and strife.
Into the expanses of space- time, they moved
learning and teaching on their way
always in the hope of the day when the power of man would be used in most effective way

Trauma

by Barry H Mansfield

＋◆◆◆◆＋

Hurtful physiological, psychological pressure causes

psychological and physiological changes,

many and varied in multiple ranges.

Some accept what society made them, a wrong occurs when there not allow or forbade,

to learn and grow in a positive way, causing a trauma that won't go away.

Making things worse

There punished and shunned because of positions they're forced to abide in.

What can be done about this terrible situation, a thing so bad it can bring down a nation.

We know that one cause of this mean degradation is a strong

fascination with power and greed, in its many manifestations.

I think what could be done with this terrible situation

is putting a stop to its primary causation.

Educating all people in righteous and productive indications

that help people grow in all of our nations.

A psychic reconstruction, cleansing the soul, introspective understanding,

of the root of the problem.

Emphasizing love and compassion and truth

is good place to start in correcting this quandary,

so, humanity could exist in harmonious peace and enlightenment,

one day.

Deceptive realities

By Barry H Mansfield

What a world we live in
taken aback in amazement,
watching in incredulous wonder
individuals of at least seemingly normal intelligence
refusing to see that which is in front of their very eyes.
Power, money, assumed revenge, seems to be their goal,
it's no joke, it's not funny,
it's a shame, it's a pity,
lies they endorse, slimy and gritty.
Truth, dignity they forbear,
oaths they swore they blatantly ignore.
If they ever had a conscience
It's nowhere to be seen
actions and words nothing but mean.
Compassion and justice not in their scene,
worst of all,
half of us seem to think it's just fine.
Society loses because they want to win,
this I perceive as an ultimate sin.

Can it be

by Barry H Mansfield

✦ ✦ ✦ ✦ ✦ ✦ ✦

Can you imagine
Souls have no gender, isn't that a wonder
they're not sexist in the least.
They make the most of whatever body they inhabit
occasionally, souls find amazing happiness in a particular gender
or they inhabit a particular gender too many times in a row
this can cause them to prefer a particular gender
causing consternation when they inhabit a particular body
not of the gender they prefer
this makes the first statement wrong
so, although a soul has no natural polarity
souls can be sexist
oh well, what do I know anyway

Don't

By Barry H Mansfield

Don't tell me you forgot already
that you, really, want to be nice.

I didn't think. You got mad
I guess you were afraid I didn't really
Love you
Now we're both really sad
Be nice I love you.

How do you know

by Barry H Mansfield

❖ ◆ ❖ ◆ ❖

I've talked about this before I'm going talk about it again.
How can you say you know? When you don't really know.
I think it's simple.
if you believe honestly, sincerely that something is or is not
if it seems to make sense in your life
and you believe with an open heart and a smile
and are brave enough to dream what you think should be
with conviction and understanding
it doesn't really matter if it is likely or unlikely
probable or improbable
keep yourself focused on where you want to go
who you want to be
so, you see
you can believe something without really knowing
and
it seems that this is the way the world works
whether for good or bad
this depends partially on intentions
and partially on research
and even with research you never really know,

Recognizing and Alleviating a Basic Flaw in Human Nature

by Barry H Mansfield

There are many individuals who have a strong desire to investigate, learn, and assimilate the most accurate information that can possibly be discerned. Most of these individuals receive little or no recognition by the mass of the population. In many cases these individuals who are actually searching for truth are ostracized by what is referred to as academia. It is truly unfortunate that in too many cases those individuals who are in charge or control of the flow of information seem to walk around with blinders on their eyes. This is a phenomenon which is a contributing factor in the inhibiting of the progressive growth of our societies.

When a large segment of society cannot and will not see relative information simply because it conflicts with previous theories, this causes a major discrepancy in our society, but not only this it also promotes the idea that it is okay to live in ignorance rather than face anything that interferes with the preconceived or current conceptions of the moment. This is demonstrated by the idea that the earth is flat and if you sail too far into the sea you will fall off the earth. Obviously, in our current timeframe we know this to be a fallacy. Yet, at one point in our history people believed this to be a fact which was justified without having any real information. Even when it was pointed out through logic and scientific methods that this is not true large segments of the population maintain this fallacy as truth.

Unfortunately, this type of hide your head in the sand belief system is still functioning to this very day. People ask for proof and even when that proof is given, they still refuse to see what is in front of their eyes and insist that what is plainly there cannot be seen. All over our planet there are sites with amazing stonework. And it truly can be seen everywhere in the world on all continent's blocks of stone so huge that we cannot conceive of how to move them even today with our modern equipment. Also, artwork in stone that if we wanted to create something similar today would take advanced planning and sophisticated tools to create the same effects. These artifacts from the past are beginning to be understood as a product of advanced civilization. There is a huge amount of this advanced work everywhere, people, look right at it, and still they can't seem to conceive that there may be a different story than the one being told.

Speaking of stories another part in this basic flaw in our society is that people except (although they claim that they don't like it) the fact that in our society lies and misconception are a major part of our commercial and political repertoire. The use of misleading or blatantly false statements is rampant within our sales and political system. And this is not restricted to large corporations or our potential political representatives. Our entire society is steeped in the usage of this misconception process to appropriate financial assets and to be in control our very lives through deception for personal gain. I could give examples and name names of institutions and individuals who perpetrate this type of deception upon us, but it is my belief that by doing so half of our population would not even pay any attention to anything I say.

Instead by just explained that this is happening I feel there is a greater possibility that more individuals will at least consider what I say. It seems that once people allow themselves to be misled, they somehow feel it is only appropriate to defend the misconceptions that are being thrust upon them or even worse that they are freely accepting these fallacies as truth. And yes, it is sometimes very difficult to figure out what is true and what is a fallacy. But I believe this could possibly be somewhat alleviated by putting more emphasis on the science or art of logic which once learned this can help differentiate between fallacy and truth.

In order to begin to alleviate this flaw in our society the individuals in our society must be educated in the art of logic, lose their inhibitions relating to the possibility of thinking for themselves rather than following the crowd.

It is only when the mass of society decides that these unrighteous detrimental actions are not to be accepted as standard policy, that then and only then can we free ourselves from this inhibiting, detrimental flaw within our society.

The Wrongs of Circumstance

by Barry H Mansfield

Discounting, karma life can sometimes be excruciatingly unfair
the silent sound, the speechless cries of agonizing torment can be felt within the air
the misery inflicted by despots of any rank are dispatched without a care
the recipients being stripped of personal power and self-will
living lives of tormented, resignation, mind- numbing frustrations,
seeing no hope to end these evil manifestations,
of corrupted power and abuse.
Still, in the very bottom of Pandora's box of misery and torment, there is still hope
our human bodies may be filled with fear, and seem unable to protest
but I still see eternal hope
within the nature of our soul, this is my belief
that throughout time there have been those
who through believe and dedication
have risen above the limitations of our fragile human forms
and have accomplished through will alone, to shine a light into the dark
reviving the human spark of dignity in truth.

Love and hate yesterday today and tomorrow!

By Barry H Mansfield

All through recorded time there has waged a conflict between love and hate. Now, in this age there are debates over whether individuals are innocent or guilty, because of actions they have taken and the results of those actions.

Society has created a very complicated legal system allowing major discrepancies in trying to judge whether actions are legal or not legal. The problem with this is it is very complicated, so let us uncomplicate the whole process we can use a much simpler method of judging an individual. A system in which clearly can be seen the process of an action and the end result of that action.

Does a person's actions display love and care for their fellow humans or does the individual's actions show mean, nasty, hurtful actions which only cause pain, frustration, humiliation, and degradation. I personally believe that seeing the difference between love and hate doesn't take a whole lot of intelligence and that it is extremely easy to see the outcome of these different ways of approaching life.

There are with us today individuals who are practitioners of love. Their actions or inactions serve one purpose and that is to bring love to their fellow human beings. There are also, individuals whose every action or inaction serve not to bring love but to bring hate, degradation, and frustration. Not to help our world and its people on the path of peace, knowledge, wisdom. Their purpose is only to cause chaos, discontent, and confusion for their own self-interest. Personally, I find the second type of individual should not be allowed in a leadership role and that all individuals who support this negative type of action are lacking severely in basic wisdom that is to say not understanding the difference between love and hate.

It seems to me, and I may be wrong, that any individual who has the smallest bit of common sense would not want to allow a truly negative or hateful individual into a position of power, and they definitely would not excuse the misuse of that power, but rather would see that this negativity, is not, productive, or beneficial in any sense and would try diligently with all their energies to stop the negativity and promote love rather than hate.

A Question of Opposites

by Barry H Mansfield

If creation is love, why is it there so much hate
there's no ignoring it, an answer must be found
are all things part of one? This seems logical to me
good and bad seem to be two half's of the whole
I see both beauty and unsightliness
and many increments in-between
there is no doubt, it's plain to see, both are there
is this fluctuating diversity insanity.
A massive battle rages inside
it pushes and pulls and paralyzes
chaos a confusion followed by clarity of mind
questions, answers for life and the divine
caught in the middle, between matter and energy's flow
a dangerous path on which to learn and grow
so many directions possible to go
disorganization, confusion tormenting my mind
still, I know that compassion and enlightenment are there for me to know
by quieting this uncertainty
accepting the love that's there is to find.

The real good news

by Barry H Mansfield

We are not born with Original Sin

but of original good

It is the guilt of our forebears that is impressed upon us that we take as our own,

that is the problem.

Wake up, break from the bad dream that is impressed upon us by those who would control.

Be still, let the incessant noise of humanity fade,

experience the silence that contains the knowledge of eternity.

We are part of it, made from it,

our ultimate potential is intertwined with it.

Rejoice, this is the good news.

The question of the suffering

by Barry H Mansfield

Humanity is quite good at suffering

also, the anticipation of suffering

the question is

is suffering beneficial

is the anticipation of suffering beneficial

yes, people get hurt

sicknesses occur

but does it help to dwell upon the problem

and more than this, to anticipate, in the future, more of the same

absolutely not

to think about the problem, or think about the problem as gone

this is the question

as I've said before and as I now repeat

the way we think controls our lives

we may not be able to control getting hurt

but fortunately, we can if we choose to, control the way we think about it

so, do not dwell upon the problem

dwell upon how good it will feel "when the problem is gone"

live your life, be happy.

Lighten the load

by Barry H Mansfield

＋＋◆◆◆＋＋

In this weighted down compressed form

that is our earthly norm

emotions are intensified

causing us to forget the true nature of our beings

we are what dreams are made of

in this reality there is nothing to be afraid of

electromagnetic fluxes held together by gravitational forces

the creativity of free will directing our courses

majestic thought mixed was a sludge of emotional confusion

can push us from hope to dissolution

so

stop and quiet your internal chatter

understand, that we are not only matter

enlightenment can be gained, from the freedom of this quiet

expanding our compression, lightening our earthly load

allowing us to transverse in glory, our paths,

on eternities road.

Community

by Barry H Mansfield

＋◆◆◆◆◆＋

We are more than our physical body
not just a commodity
the sum of our whole is much greater, we are a multicultural society
some parts weak some parts strong
what is true or right or wrong
justice is for all,
this should be our unified call,
together we stand divided we fall,
arrogant selfishness puts our backs to the wall.
Do what's right, keep universal love insight
build a world of light and hope
break through the fear of perpetual night
open your senses to the quest for true site
remember love is not demanding, it is cooperative and understanding
we can all thrive through shared participation
if we
work towards a greater integration of all the parts of our more than physical body

Better I think

by Barry H Mansfield

Better to have loved and lost, then not have loved it all
tis my belief that whoever first said this
was absolutely right.
To experience love, is a wonderful thing
and even if it does not last, it will always be there in your past
though it may have ended with a whimper
its beginning was a grand and wondrous thing
a blessing that can stay with you until the end of time
so, cherish the good, forget the bad
keep love's glow, the warmth and wonder firmly in your mind
enjoy the moments of loves first glow
this is yours forever and this you should know
it was better to have loved and lost
that never to have loved at all

The finding of true binding

by Barry H Mansfield

＊＋＊＊＋＊

Elusive and perplexing
confused with just plain sexing
the quest for true love.
Through time and space, the search goes on
looking for that special one
through a kaleidoscope of potential fun,
enjoyment and release,
but alas, not true peace.
Contentment of the soul
making half the whole.
A partnership formed in eternity
a finding that can set you free.
Soul to soul, true love you know
peace contentment and harmony
can this truly ever be
a place of ultimate reality.

"Civility for civilization

by Barry H Mansfield

Please be civil for humanity's sake

it's hard to think through an angry fog

can't see the light or know what's right

promoting unproductive useless waste of people and resources

causing a generally loathsome fate.

Try to think, be less savage,

remember the ancient adage "love your neighbor

The words they use our cosmic junk

polluting our minds like an angry skunk

sending out waves of fear and hate.

These nasty people should change their tones,

stop polluting this world with their angry funk

act with civility, one can only pray,

stop littering this world more every single day.

Sure, they're ignorant of the damage they do

(maybe)

but is this a good excuse for honking like an angry goose.

Damage goes far, deep, and wide

media blasts it, making it quite hard to hide from this polluting wake.

do yourself a favor, civility helps civilizations grow,

well, now you know, there goes your excuse.

Of the One

By Barry H. Mansfield

✦✦✦✦✦✦

We our one, We our many, We our all
That is or ever was
Creations of the cosmic mind
which is the formless creator of forms.
Let us praise the source of our creation,
by flowing through it with love and compassion.
Learning, growing, becoming more perfect in every aspect
Of our beings.
Though we may be troubled by trials and tribulations
Let us spread hope through all nations
of the possibility to form positive relations
In the name of the revelations
Of our oneness.

Birth in Death

by Barry H Mansfield

＋◆◆◆◆◆＋

Vision of realities, etched upon my mind

Staring through sight-filled eyes, totally blind

Time and space have moved apart,

Not A sound no beat of heart.

Waiting for the final play,

Which is just about to start?

Actors all aligned in transcendent majesty,

To receive their assigned parts in the rest of eternity.

So, you thought, this would-be freedom?

Oh! You thought you would be free,

Now your mind can see forever,

You know how it will be.

You can see within your very soul:

You know your destiny,

There is no place, no time or space,

Where you will ever be free!

Unless you reassess your motives,

Understand what it is you see.

Then, maybe you will notice,

You were really always free.

A reason for creation

by Barry H Mansfield

The creator infuses itself into the human being to experience its own creation

feeling the joy and wonder of that creation

in all its many manifestations

what a revelation, a cause for exaltation

we carry the spark of the creator we are touched with the divine

through us it feels the sunshine

the life-giving rain

Joy happiness, sadness pain, love, and loneliness

all over and over and over again

in the multiple aspects of its own creation

renewed it each incarnation

unending joy

fulfillment

A Matter of Matter

by Barry H Mansfield

Looking for something that doesn't seem to exist
something tenuous
that affects our reality
bends light, affects the movement of galaxies
hidden mystical mystery
something quite unknown
something like a heavy waveform
a heavy wave affected by gravity
is there a point at which the wave becomes gravity
a wave a heavy vibration
oscillating in and out of reality
energy than matter than energy than matter
affecting reality but beyond our senses
a very strange something that doesn't seem to exist,
But still affects reality.

Center of everything

by Barry H Mansfield

Where would you look if you wanted to find the center of everything
would you look inside yourself or a universe within a single cell,
a grain of sand, the consciousness of man
where would you find a center that is everywhere and nowhere
that can only be found by not looking
only by allowing yourself to be drawn to it
shattering the mirrors of our being
beyond the dreams upon dreams of our lives
a timeless state of consciousness
reached only by a balanced effort and surrender
be still and know, just let go
and you will find the center of everything.

What we truly are

by Barry H Mansfield

✦ ✦ ✦ ✦ ✦ ✦ ✦

We each are the totality of the universe
the consciousness of one is all
centered in the calm of being
a piece of the cosmic mind
infinite nonlocality, experiences
unlearn all the wrong you have learned
love to be loved
appreciate the beauty of existence
understand we're part of it
it is part of you
comprehend the I in you is part of it
it's there, find it
dwelling among the treasures in your mind

Reflection on words

by Barry H Mansfield

Do you think about what it is you say
how this affects those you meet each day
the words you give authority to
or the tone in which you speak, them
try to speak in a tone of loving care
humble up don't be gruff
don't say no, say yes and go with the flow
wisdom says let things go
words can hurt or they could heal
so, you see the things you say can really be a big deal
think and speak for goodness sake
free yourself from the bondage of negativity
be ready to be free.

I am at least partially

by Barry H Mansfield

I am what I am
energy me, matter me, love me
all I am I am
unconditional love, compassion, understanding,
open mind, and heart
this I am.
I can see with intuitive wisdom still,
I am not free to be all of that which is me.
An engine of creation with inhibitor installed
sentient being locked within itself
aware of the inhibiting force, unaware of its source
frustration and confusion blinding out the light
making it very hard to use the Inner site.
Preventing progress in the quest for understanding
enlightenment of the soul.
Still, I shall not relinquish my quest
I will work with increasing diligence to gain my final goal
disengaging the inhibitor, allowing full creative expression,
enlightenment of the soul.

As I see it

by Barry H Mansfield

◆ ◆ ◆ ◆ ◆

The deity I see, is of love, knowledge, and space- time
it's creative aspects are
life, order, the interconnectedness of all creation,
the will to keep on no matter the circumstances
the drive to love, with compassion, and understanding
to persevere against all odds,
in the quest for true knowledge of the eternal reality of truth
it's aspects reside in all of its creation
I do not believe it belongs to one group or nation
it's presence can be seen in the innumerable blazing orbs of its manifestation
at the same moment in its whirling twirling vibrations of its quantum aspects
it is all things, and we are part of it.

To know or not to know

by Barry H Mansfield

—————— ◆◆◆◆◆◆ ——————

Norms are the forms that control our lives
follow the leader is the name of their game
conform, conform let's all be the same
or get cut to pieces with their dull edge knife.
Break out of the mold that you have been placed in
see what exist that you will not face
become the instigator of the future human race.
The knowledge is there to set us all free
if you open your mind's eyes so you can see
sure, you want to keep the nonsense you been fed
and it truly is hard to get out of your head
who wants to be placed out in the cold
if you even try to break out of the conformance mold.
I sincerely think it's worth it if you give it a try
knowledge is power, I believe this is true
so, whatever happens it's all up to you

To flow

by Barry H Mansfield

◆ ◆ ◆◆◆ ◆ ◆

Energy in motion is emotion

control of this energy- emotion is a plus

it affects your mentality in this reality

this controls your vitality and your prosperity

which directs productivity and love.

How much or how little you receive is in direct proportion to the control you achieve.

Perception of time can be so subline or cause a distortion of the divine

the experience either way is the real thing

it is that, into which your life you bring

it makes you cry or lets you sing,

in that moment, it is your being

what you feel and what you're seeing

a creation of energy- emotion.

It's also true that much is hidden behind the veil we call space-time

Yes, there is a reason and oft a rhyme

behind the elusive understanding of what is on the other side of space-time.

(Change is inevitable so keep on trying)

Beauty

by Barry H Mansfield

Beauty, sensitivity, these are things I see
radiating most magnificently from the very center of thee.
If you have the time and inclination
it would be so fine
for you to sit beside me, and sip a little wine,
to entwine our fingers most gently
yours in mine,
gaze most intently into your soft warm eyes.
Reflect upon the future, the magic waiting there
yes, the many things our love could bear
if you were mine to cherish, to comfort and to hold,
my days would no longer be lonely,
my nights no longer cold.
If you would sweet lady fair, sit beside me anywhere,
The sun at Morn would shine more bright.
The stars more brilliant in the night.
The whole world would be just right, if you and I were cuddled tight.

I believe

by Barry H Mansfield

The changing

Winds

Of

time and space

form

the human race.

There is no place

or space

that is not filled with God.

So have no fear,

it is near

and never ever far.

It's okay

by Barry H Mansfield

I know that you don't believe what I believe,
and that's all right.
Still, I believe what I believe,
and that's ok!

Loves Ride

by Barry H Mansfield

* * * * *

Passions ride on loves tide

they slide and glide

sigh and cry

lie and die.

Tried, they subside,

abide and divide.

Thus, sustaining optimum duration.

Nest

by Barry H Mansfield

❖ ❖ ❖ ❖ ❖

love is a two-way street
a little nest we can sleep
feel, are toes, feet to feet
a quiet place for us to meet.

My quest

by Barry H Mansfield

◆ ◆ ◆ ◆ ◆ ◆ ◆

Where do I fit?
What is it for?
I am a being, in need of understanding
of myself and all the stimuli
that enters into my realm.
I need to grasp upon my own reality,
command to myself a new prosperity,
filled with human kindness,
and gentle serenity.
I must learn integrated sincerity,
move along a path of least resistance
to find my own true optimum potential.
This is what I need!
When I am there
my soul shall be truly free!

Ode to a goddess

by Barry H Mansfield

✦✦✦✦✦

A vision so fine, you are divine
ruby lips on mine, nectar, sweet wine
golden hair, sunshine through air
eyes like stars, diamond bright.
Every aspect of your being just right.
Love me forever, being my lady fair.
Let me love you, give me a chance to care.
Sweet moments of eternity, silver bells a chime,
ecstasy, could be ours if you were mine
Diana, virgin goddess of the hunt,
Moon goddess; shine on me your Silverlight,
that I may see to fight the loneliness which clouds my sight
allow me the love that you hold tight,
blessings saved for a wondrous night
visions of love, I see with you,
Goddess of love
My love is true

Petite lady

by Barry H Mansfield

Little lady with eyes silver blue
I'd really like to get closer to you
I can imagine the warmth of your touch,
you loving me would mean so much.
Gentle lady with eyes silver, blue,
warm and inviting smile, kind, sweet voice.
When your eyes turned towards me, and you say hello
I light up inside with a special glow
and though time and space they separate us
I want you to know, as time moves
my love will grow
Forever

Love should

by Barry H Mansfield

◆ ✦ ◆ ✦ ◆ ✦ ◆

Love should not be taken
Lightly
love should be shown, let shine
brightly
love should be shared, both day and
nightly
love should care, yes! Care most
rightly
love should be held, most gently and
tightly

Head to Heart

By Barry H Mansfield

◆ ◆ ◆ ◆ ◆

You blow my mind,
Your actions undefined,
Slow down, and love you'll find

OH! It's great to lust and fuck
But without LOVE, IT'LL BRING BAD
LUCK!

Love me slow; give our love a chance to grow,
I want you now I want you so, But Slow,
No hurry in passions haste
The years of love for us to waste

Lust and passion you can find
Greed and jealousy will blow your mind, it's
hard in this world when you want to be kind.

Life is

by Barry H Mansfield

❖ ◆ ◆ ◆ ❖

Life is strange, strange, strange,
so very hard to arrange, arrange
how much of it is actually out of your range
to re-create or rearrange?
If you think life's flow is hard to move about
you're right!
But don't give up or get uptight! Stand up straight,
begin to fight! Will things right, with all your might!
It is your right! It is your right…
Think of yourself as a shining knight
fight for your right!
But keep it light, t' is better for the site
and you will find though it is strange
there is a way to rearrange
nothing is really out of the range
you can change or re-create
all those things which we call fate
It's not too late!
Don't hesitate, or procrastinate,
why wait, time will not abate,
it is your F.A.T.E., (Excellcyate)
don't wait, you'll get things straight,
it's really… Really, not too late,
it may be strange, strange, strange,
but you can do it! Go ahead!

"TRUE, WITHOUT ERROR, CERTAIN AND MOST TRUE:
THAT WHICH IS ABOVE IS AS THAT WHICH IS BELOW,
AND THAT WHICH IS BELOW IS AS THAT WHICH IS ABOVE
FOR PERFORMING THE MIRACLES OF THE ONE THING
AND AS ALL THINGS WERE FROM ONE
BY THE MEDITATION OF ONE
SO FROM THIS ONE THING COME ALL THINGS
BY ADAPTATION."

– HERMES TRISMEGISTUS
(Emerald Tablet)

"EVERYTHING SEEN HAS BEEN BEGOTTEN
BECAUSE AT SOME POINT IT CAME TO BE SEEN.
COMING TO BE IS NOTHING BUT IMAGINATION."

– HERMES TRISMEGISTUS
Hermetica, Ch V, p18

Printed in the United States
by Baker & Taylor Publisher Services